# LEE HOIBY

# I WAS THERE

## five poems of Walt Whitman

### Baritone and Piano

ED-3829
First Printing: June 1993
Corrected Edition: February 2005

# G. SCHIRMER, Inc.

DISTRIBUTED BY

HAL•LEONARD®
CORPORATION
7777 W. BLUEMOUND RD. P.O. BOX 13819 MILWAUKEE, WI 53213

## Beginning My Studies

Beginning my studies the first step pleas'd me so much,
The mere fact consciousness, these forms, the power of motion,
The least insect or animal, the senses, eyesight, love,
The first step I say awed me and pleas'd me so much,
I have hardly gone and hardly wish'd to go any farther,
But stop and loiter all the time to sing it in ecstatic songs.


## I Was There

I understand the large hearts of heroes,
The courage of present times and all times,
How the skipper saw the crowded and rudderless wreck of the
    steam-ship, and Death chasing it up and down the storm,
How he knuckled tight and gave not back one inch, and was faithful of
    days and faithful of nights,
And chalk'd in large letters on a board, *Be of good cheer, we will not
    desert you;*
How he Follow'd with them and tack'd with them three days and would
    not give it up,
How he saved the drifting company at last,
How the lank loose-gown'd women look'd when boated from the side of
    their prepared graves,
How the silent old-faced infants, and the lifted sick, and the sharp-lipp'd
    unshaved men;
All this I swallow, it tastes good, I like it well, it becomes
    mine,
I am the man, I suffer'd, I was there.

from *Song of Myself*


## A Clear Midnight

This is thy hour O Soul, thy free flight into the wordless,
Away from books, away from art, the day erased, the lesson done,
Thee fully forth emerging, silent, gazing, pondering the themes thou
    lovest best,
Night, sleep, death and the stars.

## O Captain! My Captain!

O Captain! my Captain! our fearful trip is done,
The ship has weather'd every rack, the prize we sought is won,
The port is near, the bells I hear, the people all exulting,
While follow eyes the steady keel, the vessel grim and daring:
　But O heart! heart! heart!
　　O the bleeding drops of red,
　　　Where on the deck my Captain lies,
　　　　Fallen cold and dead.

O Captain! my Captain! rise up and hear the bells;
Rise up—for you the flag is flung—for you the bugle trills,
For you bouquets and ribbon'd wreaths—for you the shores a-crowding,
For you they call, the swaying mass, their eager faces turning;
　Here Captain! dear father!
　　This arm beneath your head!
　　　It is some dream that on the deck,
　　　　You've fallen cold and dead.

My Captain does not answer, his lips are pale and still,
My father does not feel my arm, he has no pulse nor will,
The ship is anchor'd safe and sound, its voyage closed and done,
From fearful trip the victor ship comes in with object won;
　Exult O shores, and ring O bells!
　　But I with mournful tread,
　　　Walk the deck my Captain lies,
　　　　Fallen cold and dead.


## Joy, Shipmate, Joy!

Joy, shipmate, joy!
(Pleas'd to my soul at death I cry,)
Our life is closed, our life begins,
The long, long anchorage we leave,
The ship is clear at last, she leaps!
She swiftly courses from the shore,
Joy, shipmate, joy.


I Was There *was commissioned by Peter Stewart*


*duration: ca. 15 minutes*

# I WAS THERE
## five poems of Walt Whitman

*to Hans Leder*
## 1. Beginning My Studies

Walt Whitman

Lee Hoiby

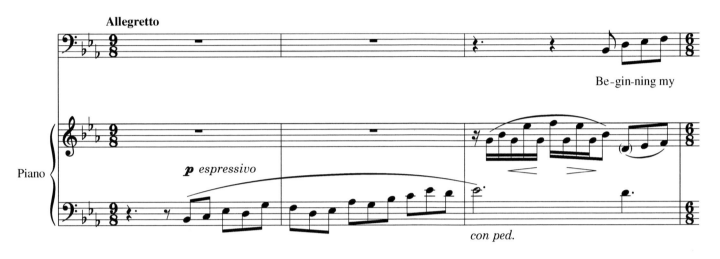

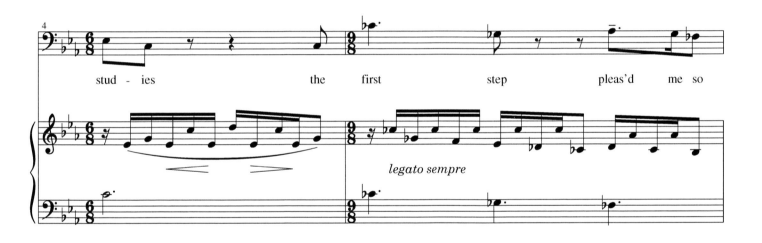

2

4

*to Eric Karpeles*

# 2. I Was There

Walt Whitman

Lee Hoiby

**Steady** ♩ = 76

Piano

*pp*

*sim.*

*poco cresc.*

*sim.*

*mp*

*pp*

I un - der - stand the

large hearts of he - roes, _____ The

*p*

cour - age of pres - ent times _____ and

knuck-led tight and gave not back one inch, and was

faith - ful of days and faith - ful of nights, and

chalked in large let-ters on a board, *Be of good*

*cheer, we will not de - sert you;* How he

*to Michael Carson*

# 3. A Clear Midnight

Walt Whitman

Lee Hoiby

12

*to Joseph Machlis*

# 4. O Captain! My Captain!

Walt Whitman

Lee Hoiby

Cap - tain, my Cap - tain! Our fear - ful trip is done. The

ship has weath-ered ev-'ry rack, the prize we sought is won, _____ The

port is near, the bells I hear, the peo - ple all ex - ult - ing. While

fol - low eyes the stead - y keel, the ves - sel grim and dar - ing;

But O _____ heart! heart!

you they call, the sway - ing mass, their ea - ger fac - es turn - ing;

Here __ Cap - tain! dear __ fa - ther! The

arm be - neath your head! It is some

dream that on this deck you've fall - en

18

*to Michael Sell*
# 5. Joy, Shipmate, Joy!

Walt Whitman

Lee Hoiby

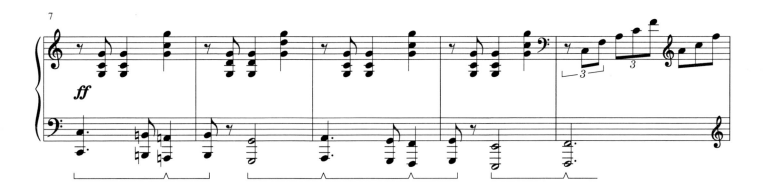

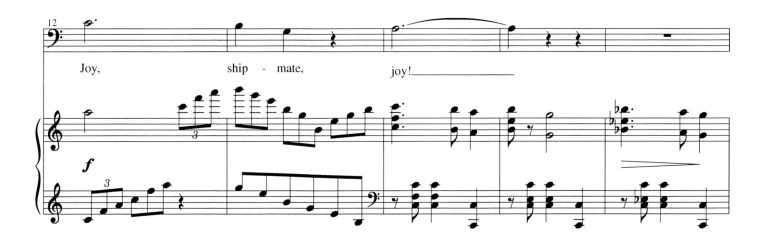

Joy,           ship - mate,        joy!_____

(Pleas'd to my soul at death I cry,) Our

life is closed, _____ our life _____

be - gins, _____

The long, long an - chor- age we

24